50 Healthy Family Meal Recipes for Home

By: Kelly Johnson

Table of Contents

- Baked Lemon Herb Salmon
- Quinoa and Black Bean Stuffed Peppers
- Grilled Chicken Salad with Mixed Greens
- Spaghetti Squash Primavera
- Turkey and Vegetable Skewers
- Lentil and Vegetable Soup
- Baked Cod with Tomato and Olive Salsa
- Vegetable Stir-Fry with Tofu
- Sweet Potato and Chickpea Curry
- Caprese Chicken Skillet
- Shrimp and Broccoli Quinoa Bowl
- Spinach and Feta Stuffed Chicken Breast
- Mediterranean Chickpea Salad
- BBQ Turkey Burgers with Avocado
- Cauliflower Fried Rice
- Baked Zucchini and Tomato Casserole
- Greek Salad with Grilled Chicken
- Eggplant Parmesan
- Pesto Zoodles with Cherry Tomatoes
- Turkey and Spinach Meatballs
- Black Bean and Corn Quesadillas
- Teriyaki Salmon Bowls with Brown Rice
- Chicken and Vegetable Kebabs
- Quinoa Salad with Roasted Vegetables
- Chickpea and Spinach Stew
- Baked Chicken Parmesan
- Asian Noodle Stir-Fry with Tofu
- Roasted Brussels Sprouts with Balsamic Glaze
- Healthy Turkey Chili
- Lemon Garlic Shrimp with Quinoa
- Cabbage and Carrot Slaw with Grilled Chicken
- Broccoli and Cheddar Stuffed Potatoes
- Turkey and Vegetable Skillet Lasagna
- Baked Pesto Chicken
- Zucchini Noodles with Tomato Sauce and Turkey Meatballs

- Grilled Veggie Quesadillas
- Sweet and Spicy Glazed Salmon
- Mediterranean Quinoa Bowl
- Chicken and Vegetable Curry
- Cauliflower and Chickpea Tacos
- Turkey and Sweet Potato Hash
- Caprese Quinoa Salad
- Lemon Garlic Roasted Chicken Thighs
- Ratatouille
- Sesame Ginger Tofu Stir-Fry
- Baked Eggplant Lasagna
- Greek Yogurt Chicken Salad Wraps
- Black Bean and Sweet Potato Enchiladas
- Pesto and Vegetable Pizza with Whole Wheat Crust
- Roasted Red Pepper and Lentil Soup

Baked Lemon Herb Salmon

Ingredients:

- 4 salmon fillets
- 2 tablespoons olive oil
- 2 cloves garlic, minced
- 1 teaspoon dried oregano
- 1 teaspoon dried thyme
- 1 teaspoon dried rosemary
- Salt and black pepper, to taste
- Zest of 1 lemon
- Juice of 1 lemon
- Fresh parsley, chopped (for garnish)

Instructions:

Preheat your oven to 400°F (200°C). Line a baking sheet with parchment paper or lightly grease it.
Place the salmon fillets on the prepared baking sheet, leaving space between each fillet.
In a small bowl, mix together the olive oil, minced garlic, dried oregano, dried thyme, dried rosemary, salt, and black pepper.
Brush the herb and oil mixture over the top of each salmon fillet, coating them evenly.
Sprinkle the lemon zest over the salmon fillets, and then drizzle the lemon juice over them.
Bake the salmon in the preheated oven for approximately 12-15 minutes or until the salmon is cooked through and easily flakes with a fork.
Optional: Broil the salmon for an additional 1-2 minutes to get a golden crust on top.
Remove the salmon from the oven and garnish with chopped fresh parsley.
Serve the Baked Lemon Herb Salmon hot, with additional lemon wedges on the side if desired.

This Baked Lemon Herb Salmon is not only delicious but also rich in omega-3 fatty acids and other essential nutrients. It pairs well with a variety of side dishes, such as steamed vegetables, quinoa, or a fresh salad. Enjoy a healthy and flavorful meal!

Quinoa and Black Bean Stuffed Peppers

Ingredients:

- 4 large bell peppers, halved and seeds removed
- 1 cup quinoa, rinsed and cooked according to package instructions
- 1 can (15 ounces) black beans, drained and rinsed
- 1 cup corn kernels (fresh, frozen, or canned)
- 1 cup diced tomatoes
- 1 cup shredded cheddar or Mexican blend cheese
- 1 teaspoon ground cumin
- 1 teaspoon chili powder
- 1/2 teaspoon smoked paprika
- Salt and black pepper, to taste
- 2 tablespoons olive oil
- Fresh cilantro, chopped, for garnish
- Sour cream or Greek yogurt, for serving (optional)

Instructions:

Preheat your oven to 375°F (190°C).
Place the halved bell peppers in a baking dish, cut side up.
In a large mixing bowl, combine the cooked quinoa, black beans, corn, diced tomatoes, shredded cheese, ground cumin, chili powder, smoked paprika, salt, and black pepper. Mix well to combine.
Drizzle the olive oil over the mixture and toss until everything is evenly coated.
Stuff each bell pepper half with the quinoa and black bean mixture, pressing down gently to pack the filling.
Cover the baking dish with aluminum foil and bake in the preheated oven for 25-30 minutes, or until the peppers are tender.
Remove the foil and bake for an additional 5-10 minutes or until the cheese is melted and bubbly.
Garnish the stuffed peppers with chopped cilantro.
Serve the Quinoa and Black Bean Stuffed Peppers hot, optionally with a dollop of sour cream or Greek yogurt on top.

These stuffed peppers are not only delicious but also a great source of plant-based protein, fiber, and various essential nutrients. They can be served as a main dish or as a side, and they're perfect for a healthy and satisfying meal. Enjoy!

Grilled Chicken Salad with Mixed Greens

Ingredients:

For the Grilled Chicken:

- 2 boneless, skinless chicken breasts
- 2 tablespoons olive oil
- 1 teaspoon dried oregano
- 1 teaspoon garlic powder
- Salt and black pepper, to taste
- Juice of 1 lemon

For the Salad:

- Mixed salad greens (e.g., spinach, arugula, romaine)
- Cherry tomatoes, halved
- Cucumber, sliced
- Red onion, thinly sliced
- Avocado, sliced
- Feta cheese, crumbled (optional)
- Balsamic vinaigrette dressing

Instructions:

Grilled Chicken:

In a bowl, mix olive oil, dried oregano, garlic powder, salt, black pepper, and lemon juice to create the marinade.
Place the chicken breasts in a shallow dish and coat them with the marinade.
Allow the chicken to marinate for at least 30 minutes, or refrigerate for a few hours for more flavor.
Preheat the grill or grill pan over medium-high heat.
Grill the chicken breasts for approximately 6-8 minutes per side or until they are fully cooked and have grill marks. The internal temperature should reach 165°F (74°C).

Remove the chicken from the grill, let it rest for a few minutes, and then slice it into thin strips.

Salad Assembly:

In a large salad bowl, combine the mixed greens, cherry tomatoes, cucumber, red onion, and avocado.
Add the grilled chicken strips on top.
Optionally, sprinkle crumbled feta cheese over the salad.
Drizzle balsamic vinaigrette dressing over the salad, tossing gently to coat all the ingredients.
Serve the Grilled Chicken Salad with Mixed Greens immediately, either as a main dish or a side.

This salad is not only delicious but also packed with protein, healthy fats, and a variety of vitamins and minerals. It's perfect for a light lunch or dinner, especially during warmer seasons. Customize the salad with your favorite vegetables and enjoy a flavorful and satisfying meal.

Spaghetti Squash Primavera

Ingredients:

- 1 medium-sized spaghetti squash
- 2 tablespoons olive oil
- 1 small red onion, thinly sliced
- 2 cloves garlic, minced
- 1 medium zucchini, julienned or thinly sliced
- 1 medium yellow squash, julienned or thinly sliced
- 1 bell pepper (red, yellow, or orange), thinly sliced
- 1 cup cherry tomatoes, halved
- 1 cup broccoli florets
- Salt and black pepper, to taste
- 1 teaspoon dried Italian herbs (thyme, oregano, basil)
- Grated Parmesan cheese, for serving (optional)
- Fresh basil or parsley, chopped, for garnish

Instructions:

Preheat your oven to 375°F (190°C).

Cut the spaghetti squash in half lengthwise and scoop out the seeds. Place the halves on a baking sheet, cut side up.

Drizzle the cut sides of the spaghetti squash with olive oil and sprinkle with salt and black pepper.

Roast the spaghetti squash in the preheated oven for 40-50 minutes or until the flesh is tender and easily shreds with a fork.

While the spaghetti squash is roasting, prepare the vegetables. In a large skillet, heat olive oil over medium heat.

Add the sliced red onion and minced garlic to the skillet, sautéing until the onion becomes translucent.

Add the julienned zucchini, yellow squash, bell pepper, cherry tomatoes, and broccoli florets to the skillet. Cook for 5-7 minutes, or until the vegetables are tender-crisp.

Season the vegetables with salt, black pepper, and dried Italian herbs. Adjust the seasoning to taste.

Once the spaghetti squash is done roasting, use a fork to scrape the flesh into "spaghetti" strands.

Add the spaghetti squash strands to the skillet with the sautéed vegetables. Toss everything together until well combined.

Serve the Spaghetti Squash Primavera hot, garnished with grated Parmesan cheese (if desired) and chopped fresh basil or parsley.

This dish is a flavorful and nutritious way to enjoy a classic primavera dish without the pasta. It's a great option for those looking to incorporate more vegetables into their meals or following a low-carb lifestyle.

Turkey and Vegetable Skewers

Ingredients:

For the Turkey Marinade:

- 1.5 pounds turkey breast or turkey tenderloins, cut into cubes
- 3 tablespoons olive oil
- 2 tablespoons soy sauce
- 1 tablespoon Dijon mustard
- 2 cloves garlic, minced
- 1 teaspoon dried thyme
- 1 teaspoon smoked paprika
- Salt and black pepper, to taste

For the Vegetable Skewers:

- Bell peppers (assorted colors), cut into chunks
- Red onion, cut into chunks
- Cherry tomatoes
- Zucchini, sliced
- Mushrooms, cleaned and halved
- Olive oil (for brushing)
- Salt and black pepper, to taste

Instructions:

In a bowl, whisk together the olive oil, soy sauce, Dijon mustard, minced garlic, dried thyme, smoked paprika, salt, and black pepper to create the marinade. Place the turkey cubes in a resealable plastic bag or a shallow dish. Pour the marinade over the turkey, ensuring that each piece is well-coated. Seal the bag or cover the dish and marinate in the refrigerator for at least 30 minutes to allow the flavors to meld.

While the turkey is marinating, soak wooden skewers in water for about 30 minutes to prevent them from burning on the grill.

Preheat the grill or grill pan over medium-high heat.

Assemble the skewers by alternating the marinated turkey cubes with chunks of bell peppers, red onion, cherry tomatoes, zucchini slices, and mushrooms.
Brush the assembled skewers with olive oil and season with salt and black pepper.
Grill the turkey and vegetable skewers for about 10-12 minutes, turning occasionally, until the turkey is cooked through and the vegetables are charred and tender.
Remove the skewers from the grill and let them rest for a few minutes.
Serve the Turkey and Vegetable Skewers hot, optionally with a side of rice, quinoa, or your favorite dipping sauce.

This dish not only provides a burst of flavors but also offers a well-balanced mix of lean protein and vegetables. It's a perfect option for a light and satisfying meal, whether you're grilling outdoors or using a grill pan indoors.

Lentil and Vegetable Soup

Ingredients:

- 1 cup dried green or brown lentils, rinsed and drained
- 2 tablespoons olive oil
- 1 onion, diced
- 2 carrots, peeled and chopped
- 2 celery stalks, chopped
- 3 cloves garlic, minced
- 1 teaspoon ground cumin
- 1 teaspoon ground coriander
- 1 teaspoon smoked paprika
- 1 bay leaf
- 1 can (14 ounces) diced tomatoes
- 6 cups vegetable or chicken broth
- Salt and black pepper, to taste
- 2 cups chopped spinach or kale
- Juice of 1 lemon
- Fresh parsley, chopped, for garnish (optional)

Instructions:

In a large pot, heat olive oil over medium heat.
Add diced onion, chopped carrots, and chopped celery. Sauté until the vegetables are softened, about 5-7 minutes.
Add minced garlic, ground cumin, ground coriander, smoked paprika, and the bay leaf. Cook for an additional 1-2 minutes, stirring to coat the vegetables in the spices.
Pour in the diced tomatoes (with their juices) and rinsed lentils. Stir to combine.
Add vegetable or chicken broth to the pot, bringing the mixture to a boil.
Reduce the heat to low, cover the pot, and let the soup simmer for about 25-30 minutes, or until the lentils are tender.
Season the soup with salt and black pepper to taste.
Add chopped spinach or kale to the pot, stirring until the greens are wilted.
Stir in the lemon juice for a bright and fresh flavor.
Remove the bay leaf before serving.

Ladle the Lentil and Vegetable Soup into bowls and garnish with chopped fresh parsley if desired.
Serve the soup hot, optionally with a side of crusty bread.

Enjoy this wholesome Lentil and Vegetable Soup as a complete and satisfying meal. It's not only delicious but also a great way to incorporate a variety of vegetables and plant-based protein into your diet.

Baked Cod with Tomato and Olive Salsa

Ingredients:

For the Baked Cod:

- 4 cod fillets
- 2 tablespoons olive oil
- 1 teaspoon paprika
- 1 teaspoon garlic powder
- Salt and black pepper, to taste
- Lemon wedges, for serving

For the Tomato and Olive Salsa:

- 1 cup cherry tomatoes, halved
- 1/2 cup Kalamata olives, pitted and sliced
- 1/4 cup red onion, finely chopped
- 2 tablespoons fresh parsley, chopped
- 1 tablespoon extra-virgin olive oil
- 1 tablespoon balsamic vinegar
- Salt and black pepper, to taste

Instructions:

Baked Cod:

Preheat your oven to 400°F (200°C).
Pat the cod fillets dry with paper towels and place them on a baking sheet lined with parchment paper.
In a small bowl, mix together olive oil, paprika, garlic powder, salt, and black pepper.
Brush the cod fillets with the olive oil mixture, ensuring they are well-coated on all sides.
Bake the cod in the preheated oven for about 12-15 minutes or until the fish is opaque and flakes easily with a fork.

Tomato and Olive Salsa:

> In a bowl, combine halved cherry tomatoes, sliced Kalamata olives, chopped red onion, and fresh parsley.
> In a separate small bowl, whisk together extra-virgin olive oil and balsamic vinegar.
> Pour the olive oil and balsamic mixture over the tomato and olive mixture. Toss to combine.
> Season the salsa with salt and black pepper to taste. Adjust the seasoning as needed.

Assembly:

> Once the cod fillets are baked, transfer them to serving plates.
> Spoon the Tomato and Olive Salsa over the top of each cod fillet.
> Serve the Baked Cod with Tomato and Olive Salsa hot, with lemon wedges on the side.

This dish is light, vibrant, and full of Mediterranean flavors. The combination of the flaky cod and the zesty salsa makes for a perfect, quick, and healthy meal. Enjoy!

Vegetable Stir-Fry with Tofu

Ingredients:

For the Tofu:

- 1 block (14-16 ounces) extra-firm tofu, pressed and cubed
- 2 tablespoons soy sauce
- 1 tablespoon cornstarch
- 1 tablespoon sesame oil
- 1 teaspoon garlic powder
- 1 teaspoon ginger powder
- 2 tablespoons vegetable oil (for cooking)

For the Stir-Fry Sauce:

- 3 tablespoons soy sauce
- 1 tablespoon hoisin sauce
- 1 tablespoon rice vinegar
- 1 tablespoon maple syrup or honey
- 1 teaspoon cornstarch

For the Vegetable Stir-Fry:

- 1 tablespoon vegetable oil
- 1 bell pepper, thinly sliced
- 1 carrot, julienned
- 1 broccoli crown, cut into florets
- 1 cup snap peas, ends trimmed
- 1 cup sliced mushrooms
- 2 green onions, chopped (for garnish)
- Sesame seeds (optional, for garnish)
- Cooked brown rice or noodles, for serving

Instructions:

Prepare the Tofu:

Press the tofu to remove excess water by placing it between two clean kitchen towels or paper towels. Place a heavy object on top and let it sit for at least 15-20 minutes.

In a bowl, mix together soy sauce, cornstarch, sesame oil, garlic powder, and ginger powder.

Cut the pressed tofu into cubes and toss them in the soy sauce mixture, ensuring each piece is well-coated.

Heat vegetable oil in a large skillet or wok over medium-high heat. Add the tofu cubes and cook until golden brown on all sides. Remove tofu from the skillet and set aside.

Prepare the Stir-Fry Sauce:

In a small bowl, whisk together soy sauce, hoisin sauce, rice vinegar, maple syrup (or honey), and cornstarch. Set aside.

Vegetable Stir-Fry:

In the same skillet or wok, add another tablespoon of vegetable oil.

Add sliced bell pepper, julienned carrot, broccoli florets, snap peas, and sliced mushrooms. Stir-fry for 5-7 minutes or until the vegetables are tender-crisp.

Return the cooked tofu to the skillet with the vegetables.

Pour the prepared stir-fry sauce over the tofu and vegetables. Toss everything together until well-coated and heated through.

Serve the Vegetable Stir-Fry with Tofu over cooked brown rice or noodles.

Garnish with chopped green onions and sesame seeds, if desired.

This Vegetable Stir-Fry with Tofu is a versatile and delicious dish that you can customize with your favorite vegetables. It's a fantastic way to enjoy a plant-based meal that's both satisfying and packed with flavor.

Sweet Potato and Chickpea Curry

Ingredients:

- 2 tablespoons vegetable oil
- 1 large onion, finely chopped
- 3 cloves garlic, minced
- 1 tablespoon fresh ginger, grated
- 2 teaspoons curry powder
- 1 teaspoon ground cumin
- 1 teaspoon ground coriander
- 1/2 teaspoon turmeric
- 1/4 teaspoon cayenne pepper (adjust to taste)
- 2 large sweet potatoes, peeled and diced
- 1 can (15 ounces) chickpeas, drained and rinsed
- 1 can (14 ounces) diced tomatoes
- 1 can (14 ounces) coconut milk
- Salt and black pepper, to taste
- Fresh cilantro, chopped (for garnish)
- Cooked basmati rice or naan bread, for serving

Instructions:

In a large pot or deep skillet, heat vegetable oil over medium heat.
Add chopped onions and sauté until they become translucent.
Stir in minced garlic and grated ginger, cooking for an additional 1-2 minutes until fragrant.
Add curry powder, ground cumin, ground coriander, turmeric, and cayenne pepper to the pot. Stir to coat the onions with the spices.
Add diced sweet potatoes to the pot and cook for 5 minutes, allowing them to slightly soften.
Pour in drained chickpeas, diced tomatoes (with their juices), and coconut milk. Stir to combine.
Season the curry with salt and black pepper to taste. Bring the mixture to a simmer.
Reduce the heat to low, cover the pot, and let it simmer for about 20-25 minutes or until the sweet potatoes are tender.
Adjust the seasoning if needed.

Serve the Sweet Potato and Chickpea Curry hot over cooked basmati rice or with naan bread.
Garnish with fresh chopped cilantro before serving.

This Sweet Potato and Chickpea Curry is a wholesome and satisfying meal. The combination of sweet potatoes and chickpeas provides a good balance of protein, fiber, and complex carbohydrates. Enjoy this flavorful curry as a comforting dinner option.

Caprese Chicken Skillet

Ingredients:

- 4 boneless, skinless chicken breasts
- Salt and black pepper, to taste
- 2 tablespoons olive oil
- 3 cloves garlic, minced
- 1 pint cherry tomatoes, halved
- 1/2 cup balsamic vinegar
- 8 ounces fresh mozzarella, sliced
- Fresh basil leaves, for garnish

Instructions:

Season the chicken breasts with salt and black pepper on both sides.
In a large skillet, heat olive oil over medium-high heat.
Add the seasoned chicken breasts to the skillet and cook for about 5-7 minutes on each side or until they are golden brown and cooked through. The internal temperature should reach 165°F (74°C).
Remove the chicken from the skillet and set it aside on a plate.
In the same skillet, add minced garlic and sauté for about 1 minute until fragrant.
Add halved cherry tomatoes to the skillet and cook for 2-3 minutes, allowing them to soften.
Pour balsamic vinegar into the skillet, stirring to combine with the tomatoes and garlic. Allow the mixture to simmer and reduce for about 5 minutes or until it thickens slightly.
Return the cooked chicken breasts to the skillet, coating them in the balsamic and tomato mixture.
Top each chicken breast with slices of fresh mozzarella.
Cover the skillet with a lid and let it cook for an additional 2-3 minutes, or until the mozzarella is melted.
Garnish the Caprese Chicken Skillet with fresh basil leaves just before serving.
Serve the chicken hot, drizzling the balsamic and tomato reduction over each piece.

This Caprese Chicken Skillet is not only visually appealing but also bursting with flavors from the tomatoes, balsamic reduction, and fresh mozzarella. It's a perfect dish for a quick and delicious dinner.

Shrimp and Broccoli Quinoa Bowl

Ingredients:

For the Quinoa:

- 1 cup quinoa, rinsed
- 2 cups water or vegetable broth
- 1/2 teaspoon salt

For the Shrimp and Broccoli:

- 1 pound large shrimp, peeled and deveined
- 2 tablespoons olive oil
- 3 cloves garlic, minced
- 1 teaspoon ginger, grated
- 4 cups broccoli florets
- Salt and black pepper, to taste
- Crushed red pepper flakes (optional, for added heat)

For the Sauce:

- 3 tablespoons soy sauce
- 2 tablespoons honey or maple syrup
- 1 tablespoon sesame oil
- 1 tablespoon rice vinegar

For Garnish:

- Sesame seeds
- Green onions, chopped
- Lime wedges

Instructions:

Quinoa:

In a medium saucepan, combine quinoa, water or vegetable broth, and salt. Bring to a boil, then reduce heat to low, cover, and simmer for 15-20 minutes or until the quinoa is cooked and the liquid is absorbed.
Fluff the quinoa with a fork and set aside.

Shrimp and Broccoli:

In a large skillet or wok, heat olive oil over medium-high heat.
Add minced garlic and grated ginger, sautéing for about 1 minute until fragrant.
Add shrimp to the skillet and cook for 2-3 minutes on each side or until they turn pink and opaque. Remove the cooked shrimp from the skillet and set aside.
In the same skillet, add broccoli florets. Cook for 3-4 minutes, or until they are tender-crisp.
Season the broccoli with salt, black pepper, and crushed red pepper flakes if desired.

Sauce:

In a small bowl, whisk together soy sauce, honey or maple syrup, sesame oil, and rice vinegar.
Pour the sauce over the broccoli in the skillet.

Assembly:

Add the cooked quinoa to the skillet with the broccoli and sauce. Toss everything together to combine.
Return the cooked shrimp to the skillet, gently folding them into the quinoa and broccoli mixture.
Cook for an additional 2-3 minutes, allowing the shrimp to heat through.
Serve the Shrimp and Broccoli Quinoa Bowl hot, garnished with sesame seeds, chopped green onions, and lime wedges.

This Shrimp and Broccoli Quinoa Bowl is a well-balanced meal with a combination of protein, vegetables, and whole grains. It's not only delicious but also a quick and healthy option for a satisfying lunch or dinner.

Spinach and Feta Stuffed Chicken Breast

Ingredients:

- 4 boneless, skinless chicken breasts
- Salt and black pepper, to taste
- 2 tablespoons olive oil
- 2 cloves garlic, minced
- 4 cups fresh spinach, chopped
- 1/2 cup feta cheese, crumbled
- 1/4 cup sun-dried tomatoes, chopped (optional)
- 1 teaspoon dried oregano
- 1 teaspoon dried thyme
- 1 teaspoon paprika
- Toothpicks or kitchen twine (optional)

Instructions:

Preheat the oven to 375°F (190°C).
Season the chicken breasts with salt and black pepper on both sides.
In a large skillet, heat olive oil over medium heat.
Add minced garlic to the skillet and sauté for about 1 minute until fragrant.
Add chopped spinach to the skillet and cook until wilted, about 2-3 minutes.
Remove the skillet from the heat and stir in crumbled feta cheese, sun-dried tomatoes (if using), dried oregano, dried thyme, and paprika. Mix until well combined.
Make a horizontal slit in each chicken breast to create a pocket for the stuffing. Be careful not to cut all the way through.
Stuff each chicken breast with the spinach and feta mixture, pressing it gently to pack the filling.
If desired, use toothpicks or kitchen twine to secure the edges of the chicken breasts and keep the stuffing in place.
Season the outside of the stuffed chicken breasts with a bit more salt and pepper.
Heat a bit more olive oil in the skillet over medium-high heat. Brown the stuffed chicken breasts for 2-3 minutes on each side.

Transfer the browned chicken breasts to a baking dish and bake in the preheated oven for about 20-25 minutes or until the chicken is cooked through and reaches an internal temperature of 165°F (74°C).
Remove the toothpicks or twine before serving.
Serve the Spinach and Feta Stuffed Chicken Breast hot, optionally garnished with fresh herbs or a squeeze of lemon.

This dish not only looks impressive but also offers a delightful combination of flavors.

Enjoy the succulent chicken with the savory spinach and feta filling for a satisfying and flavorful meal.

Mediterranean Chickpea Salad

Ingredients:

For the Salad:

- 2 cans (15 ounces each) chickpeas, drained and rinsed
- 1 cucumber, diced
- 1 cup cherry tomatoes, halved
- 1 red bell pepper, diced
- 1/2 red onion, finely chopped
- 1/2 cup Kalamata olives, pitted and sliced
- 1/2 cup feta cheese, crumbled
- Fresh parsley, chopped, for garnish

For the Dressing:

- 1/4 cup extra-virgin olive oil
- 2 tablespoons red wine vinegar
- 1 teaspoon Dijon mustard
- 1 clove garlic, minced
- 1 teaspoon dried oregano
- Salt and black pepper, to taste

Instructions:

In a large salad bowl, combine chickpeas, diced cucumber, cherry tomatoes, diced red bell pepper, finely chopped red onion, sliced Kalamata olives, and crumbled feta cheese.
In a small bowl, whisk together extra-virgin olive oil, red wine vinegar, Dijon mustard, minced garlic, dried oregano, salt, and black pepper to create the dressing.
Pour the dressing over the salad and toss gently to coat all the ingredients.
Allow the Mediterranean Chickpea Salad to sit for at least 15-20 minutes before serving to let the flavors meld.
Garnish the salad with freshly chopped parsley just before serving.
Serve the Mediterranean Chickpea Salad chilled as a side dish or a light and healthy main course.

This salad is not only colorful and vibrant but also rich in protein, fiber, and healthy fats. It's perfect for picnics, potlucks, or as a refreshing side dish for any meal. Enjoy the Mediterranean flavors!

BBQ Turkey Burgers with Avocado

Ingredients:

For the Turkey Burgers:

- 1 pound ground turkey
- 1/4 cup breadcrumbs
- 1/4 cup barbecue sauce (plus extra for brushing)
- 1 teaspoon onion powder
- 1 teaspoon garlic powder
- Salt and black pepper, to taste
- 4 whole wheat burger buns

For Topping:

- 2 avocados, sliced
- Lettuce leaves
- Tomato slices
- Red onion slices

Instructions:

In a large bowl, combine ground turkey, breadcrumbs, barbecue sauce, onion powder, garlic powder, salt, and black pepper. Mix until all ingredients are well combined.

Divide the turkey mixture into four equal portions and shape them into burger patties.

Preheat your grill or grill pan over medium-high heat.

Place the turkey burgers on the preheated grill and cook for about 5-6 minutes per side or until they are fully cooked and reach an internal temperature of 165°F (74°C).

Brush the burgers with additional barbecue sauce during the last few minutes of grilling for extra flavor.

While the burgers are cooking, slice the avocado, lettuce, tomatoes, and red onion.

Toast the whole wheat burger buns on the grill for a minute or until lightly browned.
Assemble the BBQ Turkey Burgers by placing each cooked patty on a toasted bun.
Top each burger with avocado slices, lettuce, tomato, and red onion.
Serve the BBQ Turkey Burgers with Avocado hot and enjoy!

These BBQ Turkey Burgers with Avocado are not only tasty but also a healthier option with lean turkey and the creamy goodness of avocado. Customize the toppings to your liking and savor a delicious and satisfying meal.

Cauliflower Fried Rice

Ingredients:

- 1 medium-sized cauliflower, grated or processed into rice-sized pieces
- 2 tablespoons vegetable oil
- 2 cloves garlic, minced
- 1 tablespoon ginger, grated
- 1 cup mixed vegetables (peas, carrots, corn, diced bell peppers, etc.)
- 2 green onions, sliced
- 2 eggs, beaten (optional)
- 3 tablespoons soy sauce
- 1 tablespoon sesame oil
- Salt and black pepper, to taste
- Chopped cilantro or parsley for garnish (optional)

Instructions:

Grate the cauliflower using a box grater or pulse it in a food processor until it resembles rice-sized grains.
Heat vegetable oil in a large skillet or wok over medium-high heat.
Add minced garlic and grated ginger to the hot oil. Sauté for about 1 minute until fragrant.
Add the mixed vegetables to the skillet and stir-fry for 3-4 minutes until they are slightly tender.
Push the vegetables to one side of the skillet, creating space for the eggs (if using). Pour the beaten eggs into the empty side of the skillet and scramble them until cooked.
Combine the scrambled eggs with the vegetables.
Add the grated cauliflower to the skillet, mixing well with the vegetables and eggs.
Pour soy sauce and sesame oil over the cauliflower mixture. Stir to coat evenly.
Season the Cauliflower Fried Rice with salt and black pepper to taste.
Cook for an additional 5-7 minutes, stirring frequently, until the cauliflower is cooked but still has a slight crunch.
Stir in sliced green onions and garnish with chopped cilantro or parsley if desired.
Serve the Cauliflower Fried Rice hot as a side dish or a main course.

This Cauliflower Fried Rice is a flavorful and satisfying option for those looking to reduce their carbohydrate intake or incorporate more vegetables into their meals. Customize the ingredients to suit your taste and enjoy a tasty and healthy alternative to traditional fried rice.

Greek Salad with Grilled Chicken

Ingredients:

For the Grilled Chicken:

- 4 boneless, skinless chicken breasts
- 2 tablespoons olive oil
- 1 teaspoon dried oregano
- 1 teaspoon dried thyme
- 1 teaspoon garlic powder
- Salt and black pepper, to taste
- Juice of 1 lemon

For the Greek Salad:

- 1 large cucumber, diced
- 1 cup cherry tomatoes, halved
- 1 red bell pepper, diced
- 1/2 red onion, thinly sliced
- 1 cup Kalamata olives, pitted
- 1 cup feta cheese, crumbled
- Fresh parsley, chopped, for garnish

For the Greek Salad Dressing:

- 1/4 cup extra-virgin olive oil
- 2 tablespoons red wine vinegar
- 1 teaspoon Dijon mustard
- 1 clove garlic, minced
- 1 teaspoon dried oregano
- Salt and black pepper, to taste

Instructions:

Grilled Chicken:

In a bowl, mix together olive oil, dried oregano, dried thyme, garlic powder, salt, black pepper, and lemon juice to create the marinade.

Place the chicken breasts in a shallow dish and coat them with the marinade. Allow the chicken to marinate for at least 30 minutes, or refrigerate for a few hours for more flavor.

Preheat the grill or grill pan over medium-high heat.

Grill the chicken breasts for approximately 6-8 minutes per side or until they are fully cooked and have grill marks. The internal temperature should reach 165°F (74°C).

Remove the chicken from the grill, let it rest for a few minutes, and then slice it into thin strips.

Greek Salad:

In a large salad bowl, combine diced cucumber, halved cherry tomatoes, diced red bell pepper, thinly sliced red onion, pitted Kalamata olives, and crumbled feta cheese.

In a small bowl, whisk together extra-virgin olive oil, red wine vinegar, Dijon mustard, minced garlic, dried oregano, salt, and black pepper to create the dressing.

Pour the dressing over the salad and toss gently to coat all the ingredients.

Top the Greek Salad with the sliced grilled chicken.

Garnish the salad with fresh chopped parsley.

Serve the Greek Salad with Grilled Chicken immediately as a light and satisfying meal.

This Greek Salad with Grilled Chicken is a perfect balance of fresh vegetables, tangy feta cheese, and savory grilled chicken, all enhanced by the classic flavors of Greek cuisine. Enjoy this wholesome and flavorful dish!

Eggplant Parmesan

Ingredients:

- 2 large eggplants, sliced into 1/2-inch rounds
- Salt, for sweating the eggplant
- 2 cups all-purpose flour, for dredging
- 4 large eggs, beaten
- 2 cups Italian-style breadcrumbs
- 1 cup grated Parmesan cheese
- Olive oil, for frying
- 4 cups marinara sauce (homemade or store-bought)
- 2 cups shredded mozzarella cheese
- Fresh basil or parsley, chopped, for garnish

Instructions:

Preheat the oven to 375°F (190°C).
Place the eggplant slices on a paper towel-lined surface and sprinkle both sides with salt. Allow them to sit for about 30 minutes to draw out excess moisture. This step helps reduce bitterness and prevents the eggplant from becoming soggy during cooking.
In three separate shallow dishes, place the flour in one, beaten eggs in another, and a mixture of breadcrumbs and grated Parmesan cheese in the third.
Heat olive oil in a large skillet over medium-high heat.
Dredge each eggplant slice in the flour, dip it into the beaten eggs, and coat it with the breadcrumb-Parmesan mixture, pressing the breadcrumbs onto the eggplant to adhere.
Fry the breaded eggplant slices in the hot oil until golden brown on both sides.
Transfer them to a paper towel-lined plate to drain excess oil.
In a baking dish, spread a thin layer of marinara sauce.
Arrange a layer of fried eggplant slices on top of the sauce.
Repeat the layers, finishing with a layer of marinara sauce on top.
Sprinkle shredded mozzarella cheese over the final layer.
Bake in the preheated oven for 25-30 minutes or until the cheese is melted and bubbly.
Remove from the oven and let it rest for a few minutes before serving.
Garnish with fresh chopped basil or parsley before serving.

Serve the Eggplant Parmesan hot as a main dish, optionally over cooked pasta or with a side of crusty bread.

This Eggplant Parmesan is a comforting and hearty dish that showcases the wonderful flavors of eggplant and marinara sauce. Enjoy the crispy, golden exterior and the cheesy goodness of this classic Italian favorite.

Pesto Zoodles with Cherry Tomatoes

Ingredients:

For the Pesto:

- 2 cups fresh basil leaves, packed
- 1/2 cup grated Parmesan cheese
- 1/3 cup pine nuts or walnuts
- 3 cloves garlic, minced
- 1/2 cup extra-virgin olive oil
- Salt and black pepper, to taste

For the Zoodles:

- 4 medium-sized zucchini, spiralized into noodles
- 1 tablespoon olive oil
- 1 pint cherry tomatoes, halved
- Salt and black pepper, to taste
- Grated Parmesan cheese, for garnish
- Fresh basil leaves, for garnish

Instructions:

Pesto:

In a food processor, combine fresh basil, grated Parmesan cheese, pine nuts (or walnuts), and minced garlic.
Pulse the ingredients until coarsely chopped.
With the food processor running, gradually add the olive oil in a steady stream until the pesto reaches your desired consistency.
Season the pesto with salt and black pepper to taste. Set aside.

Zoodles:

Spiralize the zucchini into noodles using a spiralizer.
In a large skillet, heat olive oil over medium heat.

Add the zucchini noodles to the skillet and toss for 2-3 minutes until they are just tender. Be careful not to overcook, as zoodles can become mushy.

Add the halved cherry tomatoes to the skillet and toss for an additional 1-2 minutes until they are heated through.

Stir in the prepared pesto, ensuring the zoodles and tomatoes are well coated. Season with salt and black pepper to taste.

Remove the skillet from the heat.

Serve the Pesto Zoodles with Cherry Tomatoes hot, garnished with grated Parmesan cheese and fresh basil leaves.

This Pesto Zoodles with Cherry Tomatoes recipe is not only quick and easy but also a perfect way to enjoy a light and flavorful meal. The freshness of the vegetables combined with the vibrant pesto makes for a delightful and nutritious dish.

Turkey and Spinach Meatballs

Ingredients:

- 1 pound ground turkey
- 1 cup fresh spinach, finely chopped
- 1/2 cup breadcrumbs
- 1/4 cup grated Parmesan cheese
- 1/4 cup finely chopped onion
- 2 cloves garlic, minced
- 1 large egg
- 1 teaspoon dried oregano
- 1 teaspoon dried basil
- 1/2 teaspoon salt
- 1/4 teaspoon black pepper
- Olive oil, for cooking

Instructions:

Preheat the oven to 375°F (190°C).

In a large mixing bowl, combine ground turkey, chopped spinach, breadcrumbs, Parmesan cheese, chopped onion, minced garlic, egg, dried oregano, dried basil, salt, and black pepper.

Mix the ingredients until well combined. Be careful not to overmix to maintain a tender texture.

Shape the mixture into meatballs, about 1 to 1.5 inches in diameter, and place them on a baking sheet lined with parchment paper.

Heat olive oil in a large skillet over medium-high heat.

Brown the meatballs on all sides in the skillet, working in batches if necessary. This step is to sear the meatballs, and they will finish cooking in the oven.

Transfer the browned meatballs back to the baking sheet.

Bake in the preheated oven for 15-20 minutes or until the internal temperature reaches 165°F (74°C) and the meatballs are cooked through.

Remove from the oven and let them rest for a few minutes before serving.

Serve the Turkey and Spinach Meatballs with your favorite sauce, pasta, or as desired.

These Turkey and Spinach Meatballs are a nutritious and flavorful option, and they're versatile enough to be enjoyed in various dishes. Whether you pair them with pasta, use them in sandwiches, or serve them with a dipping sauce, these meatballs make for a tasty and wholesome meal.

Black Bean and Corn Quesadillas

Ingredients:

- 1 can (15 ounces) black beans, drained and rinsed
- 1 cup corn kernels (fresh, frozen, or canned)
- 1 cup shredded cheese (cheddar, Monterey Jack, or a blend)
- 1/2 cup diced red bell pepper
- 1/4 cup chopped fresh cilantro
- 1 teaspoon ground cumin
- 1/2 teaspoon chili powder
- Salt and black pepper, to taste
- 4 large flour tortillas
- Olive oil, for cooking
- Salsa, guacamole, or sour cream for serving (optional)

Instructions:

In a medium bowl, combine black beans, corn, shredded cheese, diced red bell pepper, chopped cilantro, ground cumin, chili powder, salt, and black pepper. Mix well to ensure even distribution of ingredients.

Lay out the flour tortillas on a clean surface.

Divide the black bean and corn mixture evenly among half of each tortilla, leaving the other half empty.

Fold the tortillas over to create half-moon shapes, pressing down gently to secure the filling.

Heat a skillet or griddle over medium heat. Brush the surface with a small amount of olive oil.

Place the quesadillas on the hot surface and cook for 2-3 minutes on each side or until the tortillas are golden brown, and the cheese is melted.

Remove the quesadillas from the skillet and let them rest for a minute before slicing.

Repeat the process with the remaining quesadillas.

Slice each quesadilla into wedges and serve hot.

Optionally, serve the Black Bean and Corn Quesadillas with salsa, guacamole, or sour cream on the side.

These Black Bean and Corn Quesadillas are a versatile and flavorful option. They can be enjoyed as a quick lunch, dinner, or even as a party snack. Customize the filling with your favorite ingredients to make it your own.

Teriyaki Salmon Bowls with Brown Rice

Ingredients:

For the Teriyaki Salmon:

- 4 salmon fillets
- 1/4 cup soy sauce
- 2 tablespoons mirin (sweet rice wine)
- 2 tablespoons honey
- 1 tablespoon rice vinegar
- 1 teaspoon sesame oil
- 2 cloves garlic, minced
- 1 teaspoon grated ginger
- Sesame seeds, for garnish
- Green onions, chopped, for garnish

For the Brown Rice:

- 2 cups cooked brown rice

For the Vegetable Toppings:

- 2 cups broccoli florets, steamed
- 1 bell pepper, thinly sliced
- 1 carrot, julienned
- 1 cucumber, thinly sliced
- Avocado slices, for garnish

Instructions:

Teriyaki Salmon:

In a bowl, whisk together soy sauce, mirin, honey, rice vinegar, sesame oil, minced garlic, and grated ginger to create the teriyaki sauce.
Place the salmon fillets in a shallow dish and pour half of the teriyaki sauce over them. Allow the salmon to marinate for at least 15-30 minutes.

Preheat the oven to 400°F (200°C).

Transfer the marinated salmon fillets to a baking sheet lined with parchment paper.

Bake in the preheated oven for 12-15 minutes or until the salmon is cooked through and flakes easily with a fork.

During the last few minutes of baking, brush the salmon with the remaining teriyaki sauce.

Remove the salmon from the oven and sprinkle with sesame seeds and chopped green onions.

Bowls Assembly:

Divide cooked brown rice among serving bowls.

Top the rice with steamed broccoli florets, sliced bell pepper, julienned carrot, and cucumber slices.

Place a teriyaki-glazed salmon fillet on top of the vegetables in each bowl.

Garnish with avocado slices.

Drizzle any remaining teriyaki sauce over the bowls.

Serve the Teriyaki Salmon Bowls hot, optionally garnished with additional sesame seeds and green onions.

These Teriyaki Salmon Bowls with Brown Rice are a nutritious and flavorful meal, combining the goodness of salmon, brown rice, and colorful vegetables. The homemade teriyaki sauce adds a perfect balance of sweet and savory flavors. Enjoy this delicious and well-balanced dish for a satisfying dinner.

Chicken and Vegetable Kebabs

Ingredients:

For the Marinade:

- 1.5 pounds boneless, skinless chicken breasts, cut into chunks
- 1/4 cup olive oil
- 3 tablespoons soy sauce
- 2 tablespoons honey
- 2 cloves garlic, minced
- 1 teaspoon ground cumin
- 1 teaspoon paprika
- 1/2 teaspoon black pepper
- 1/2 teaspoon dried oregano
- Juice of 1 lemon

For the Kebabs:

- Bell peppers, cut into chunks (assorted colors)
- Cherry tomatoes
- Red onion, cut into chunks
- Zucchini, sliced

Wooden or metal skewers

Instructions:

In a bowl, whisk together olive oil, soy sauce, honey, minced garlic, ground cumin, paprika, black pepper, dried oregano, and lemon juice to create the marinade.
Place the chicken chunks in a zip-top bag or a shallow dish. Pour half of the marinade over the chicken, reserving the rest for basting.
Seal the bag or cover the dish and let the chicken marinate in the refrigerator for at least 30 minutes or up to 4 hours.
If using wooden skewers, soak them in water for about 30 minutes to prevent burning during grilling.
Preheat the grill to medium-high heat.

Thread marinated chicken chunks, bell pepper chunks, cherry tomatoes, red onion chunks, and zucchini slices onto the skewers, alternating between the chicken and vegetables.

Brush the kebabs with the reserved marinade.

Place the skewers on the preheated grill and cook for about 10-15 minutes, turning occasionally, until the chicken is cooked through and the vegetables are tender and lightly charred.

Baste the kebabs with the marinade during the last few minutes of grilling for added flavor.

Remove the kebabs from the grill and let them rest for a few minutes before serving.

Serve the Chicken and Vegetable Kebabs hot, optionally garnished with chopped fresh herbs like parsley or cilantro.

These Chicken and Vegetable Kebabs are not only visually appealing but also packed with delicious flavors. Enjoy them as a main course with a side of rice or a fresh salad for a wholesome and satisfying meal.

Quinoa Salad with Roasted Vegetables

Ingredients:

For the Salad:

- 1 cup quinoa, rinsed
- 2 cups water or vegetable broth
- 1 cup cherry tomatoes, halved
- 1 medium red bell pepper, diced
- 1 medium yellow bell pepper, diced
- 1 medium zucchini, diced
- 1 small red onion, thinly sliced
- 1 cup broccoli florets
- 2 tablespoons olive oil
- Salt and black pepper, to taste
- 1/4 cup crumbled feta cheese (optional)
- Fresh parsley, chopped, for garnish

For the Dressing:

- 1/4 cup extra-virgin olive oil
- 2 tablespoons balsamic vinegar
- 1 teaspoon Dijon mustard
- 1 clove garlic, minced
- Salt and black pepper, to taste

Instructions:

Roasted Vegetables:

Preheat the oven to 400°F (200°C).
In a large bowl, combine the diced red and yellow bell peppers, cherry tomatoes, zucchini, red onion, and broccoli florets.
Drizzle the vegetables with 2 tablespoons of olive oil, and season with salt and black pepper. Toss to coat the vegetables evenly.
Spread the vegetables in a single layer on a baking sheet lined with parchment paper.
Roast in the preheated oven for 20-25 minutes or until the vegetables are tender and slightly caramelized, stirring once halfway through.

Remove the roasted vegetables from the oven and let them cool.

Quinoa:

In a medium saucepan, combine quinoa and water or vegetable broth. Bring to a boil, then reduce heat to low, cover, and simmer for 15-20 minutes or until the quinoa is cooked and the liquid is absorbed.
Fluff the quinoa with a fork and let it cool.

Dressing:

In a small bowl, whisk together extra-virgin olive oil, balsamic vinegar, Dijon mustard, minced garlic, salt, and black pepper to create the dressing.

Assembly:

In a large serving bowl, combine the cooked quinoa, roasted vegetables, and crumbled feta cheese (if using).
Pour the dressing over the salad and toss gently to coat all the ingredients.
Garnish with chopped fresh parsley.
Serve the Quinoa Salad with Roasted Vegetables at room temperature or chilled.

This Quinoa Salad with Roasted Vegetables is not only a great side dish but also a satisfying and nutritious main course. The combination of quinoa and colorful roasted vegetables creates a tasty and wholesome meal that can be enjoyed on its own or as a side to grilled chicken or fish.

Chickpea and Spinach Stew

Ingredients:

- 2 tablespoons olive oil
- 1 onion, finely chopped
- 3 cloves garlic, minced
- 1 teaspoon ground cumin
- 1 teaspoon ground coriander
- 1/2 teaspoon smoked paprika
- 1/4 teaspoon cayenne pepper (optional, for heat)
- 1 can (15 ounces) chickpeas, drained and rinsed
- 1 can (14 ounces) diced tomatoes
- 1 cup vegetable broth
- 1 teaspoon dried thyme
- Salt and black pepper, to taste
- 6 cups fresh spinach leaves, washed and chopped
- Juice of 1 lemon
- Fresh cilantro or parsley, chopped, for garnish

Instructions:

In a large pot or Dutch oven, heat olive oil over medium heat.
Add chopped onion and sauté until translucent, about 5 minutes.
Stir in minced garlic and cook for an additional 1-2 minutes until fragrant.
Add ground cumin, ground coriander, smoked paprika, and cayenne pepper (if using). Stir to coat the onions and garlic with the spices.
Pour in the diced tomatoes, chickpeas, vegetable broth, dried thyme, salt, and black pepper. Bring the mixture to a simmer.
Cover the pot and let the stew simmer for 15-20 minutes to allow the flavors to meld.
Add the chopped spinach to the stew, stirring until it wilts into the mixture.
Squeeze the juice of one lemon into the stew and stir.
Adjust the seasoning to taste, adding more salt, pepper, or lemon juice if needed.
Let the Chickpea and Spinach Stew cook for an additional 5 minutes to ensure the spinach is fully cooked.
Remove the pot from the heat.
Serve the stew hot, garnished with fresh cilantro or parsley.

This Chickpea and Spinach Stew is not only delicious but also a great source of plant-based protein and fiber. Enjoy it as a filling and nutritious meal on its own or pair it with your favorite bread or rice.

Baked Chicken Parmesan

Ingredients:

For the Chicken:

- 4 boneless, skinless chicken breasts
- Salt and black pepper, to taste
- 1 cup all-purpose flour
- 2 large eggs, beaten
- 1 cup Italian-style breadcrumbs
- 1/2 cup grated Parmesan cheese
- Cooking spray or olive oil for baking

For the Assembly:

- 2 cups marinara sauce (homemade or store-bought)
- 1 cup shredded mozzarella cheese
- 1/4 cup grated Parmesan cheese
- Fresh basil or parsley, chopped, for garnish

Instructions:

Preheat the oven to 400°F (200°C). Line a baking sheet with parchment paper or lightly grease it with cooking spray.

Season each chicken breast with salt and black pepper on both sides.

Set up a breading station with three shallow bowls: one with flour, one with beaten eggs, and one with a mixture of breadcrumbs and grated Parmesan cheese.

Dredge each chicken breast in the flour, shaking off any excess. Dip it into the beaten eggs, allowing any excess to drip off. Finally, coat the chicken in the breadcrumb-Parmesan mixture, pressing the breadcrumbs onto the chicken to adhere.

Place the breaded chicken breasts on the prepared baking sheet.

Lightly spray the top of each chicken breast with cooking spray or drizzle with a bit of olive oil. This helps them crisp up during baking.

Bake in the preheated oven for 20-25 minutes or until the chicken is cooked through and the crust is golden brown and crispy.

Remove the chicken from the oven and spoon marinara sauce over each piece.
Sprinkle shredded mozzarella and grated Parmesan cheese over the top.
Return the chicken to the oven and bake for an additional 10 minutes or until the cheese is melted and bubbly.
Garnish with chopped fresh basil or parsley before serving.
Serve the Baked Chicken Parmesan hot over pasta, rice, or a bed of fresh greens.

This Baked Chicken Parmesan is a lighter version of the classic dish, and it still delivers the comforting flavors of crispy chicken, rich marinara sauce, and melted cheese. Enjoy this delicious and satisfying meal!

Asian Noodle Stir-Fry with Tofu

Ingredients:

- 8 oz (about 225g) rice noodles or any Asian noodles of your choice
- 1 block firm tofu, pressed and cubed
- 2 tablespoons soy sauce
- 2 tablespoons hoisin sauce
- 1 tablespoon sesame oil
- 1 tablespoon rice vinegar
- 1 tablespoon maple syrup or brown sugar
- 2 tablespoons vegetable oil
- 3 cloves garlic, minced
- 1 tablespoon ginger, grated
- 1 bell pepper, thinly sliced
- 1 carrot, julienned
- 1 cup broccoli florets
- 1 cup snap peas, trimmed
- 2 green onions, sliced
- Sesame seeds and chopped cilantro for garnish (optional)

Instructions:

Cook the rice noodles according to the package instructions. Drain and set aside. In a bowl, mix together soy sauce, hoisin sauce, sesame oil, rice vinegar, and maple syrup (or brown sugar) to create the stir-fry sauce. Set aside.

Press the tofu to remove excess water and cut it into cubes. Toss the tofu cubes with 2 tablespoons of soy sauce and set aside to marinate.

Heat 1 tablespoon of vegetable oil in a large wok or skillet over medium-high heat.

Add the marinated tofu to the wok and cook until the tofu is golden brown on all sides. Remove the tofu from the wok and set it aside.

In the same wok, add another tablespoon of vegetable oil.

Add minced garlic and grated ginger to the wok, sautéing for about 30 seconds until fragrant.

Add the sliced bell pepper, julienned carrot, broccoli florets, and snap peas to the wok. Stir-fry the vegetables for 3-4 minutes until they are crisp-tender.

Return the cooked tofu to the wok and add the cooked rice noodles.

Pour the stir-fry sauce over the noodles and tofu, tossing everything together until well coated and heated through.
Add sliced green onions and toss briefly.
Garnish with sesame seeds and chopped cilantro if desired.
Serve the Asian Noodle Stir-Fry with Tofu hot and enjoy!

This Asian Noodle Stir-Fry with Tofu is a versatile dish, and you can customize the vegetables and noodles according to your preferences. The flavorful sauce and the combination of tofu and vegetables make it a delicious and satisfying meal.

Roasted Brussels Sprouts with Balsamic Glaze

Ingredients:

- 1 pound Brussels sprouts, trimmed and halved
- 2 tablespoons olive oil
- Salt and black pepper, to taste
- 2 tablespoons balsamic glaze (store-bought or homemade)
- Optional: Grated Parmesan cheese for garnish

Instructions:

Preheat the oven to 400°F (200°C). Line a baking sheet with parchment paper for easy cleanup.
In a large bowl, toss the halved Brussels sprouts with olive oil until they are well coated.
Season the Brussels sprouts with salt and black pepper to taste.
Spread the Brussels sprouts evenly on the prepared baking sheet.
Roast in the preheated oven for 20-25 minutes or until the Brussels sprouts are golden brown and crispy on the edges. Be sure to stir or shake the pan halfway through to ensure even roasting.
Remove the Brussels sprouts from the oven and transfer them to a serving dish.
Drizzle the balsamic glaze over the roasted Brussels sprouts.
If desired, sprinkle grated Parmesan cheese over the top for added flavor.
Toss the Brussels sprouts gently to coat them with the balsamic glaze.
Serve the Roasted Brussels Sprouts with Balsamic Glaze immediately as a flavorful side dish.

This dish is a great way to enjoy Brussels sprouts with minimal effort. The roasting process enhances the natural sweetness of the Brussels sprouts, and the balsamic glaze adds a delightful tangy flavor. Serve it alongside your favorite main course for a tasty and nutritious meal.

Healthy Turkey Chili

Ingredients:

- 1 tablespoon olive oil
- 1 large onion, diced
- 3 cloves garlic, minced
- 1 pound ground turkey (93% lean or leaner)
- 1 bell pepper, diced (any color)
- 1 zucchini, diced
- 1 carrot, diced
- 1 can (15 ounces) black beans, drained and rinsed
- 1 can (15 ounces) kidney beans, drained and rinsed
- 1 can (28 ounces) diced tomatoes (fire-roasted, if available)
- 1 cup corn kernels (fresh, frozen, or canned)
- 2 cups low-sodium chicken broth
- 2 tablespoons tomato paste
- 2 teaspoons chili powder
- 1 teaspoon ground cumin
- 1/2 teaspoon paprika
- 1/2 teaspoon dried oregano
- 1/2 teaspoon ground coriander
- Salt and black pepper, to taste
- Optional toppings: shredded cheese, Greek yogurt or sour cream, chopped green onions, cilantro, lime wedges

Instructions:

In a large pot or Dutch oven, heat olive oil over medium heat.
Add diced onion and cook until softened, about 5 minutes.
Add minced garlic and cook for an additional 1-2 minutes until fragrant.
Add ground turkey to the pot and cook until browned, breaking it apart with a spoon as it cooks.
Stir in diced bell pepper, zucchini, and carrot. Cook for 3-4 minutes until the vegetables begin to soften.
Add black beans, kidney beans, diced tomatoes, corn, chicken broth, and tomato paste to the pot. Stir to combine.

Season the chili with chili powder, ground cumin, paprika, dried oregano, ground coriander, salt, and black pepper. Adjust the seasonings to taste.

Bring the chili to a simmer, then reduce the heat to low, cover, and let it simmer for 30-40 minutes, allowing the flavors to meld.

Serve the Healthy Turkey Chili hot, garnished with your favorite toppings such as shredded cheese, Greek yogurt or sour cream, chopped green onions, cilantro, and lime wedges.

This Healthy Turkey Chili is not only delicious but also a great source of lean protein and fiber. It's a wholesome and satisfying meal that's perfect for cozy evenings. Feel free to customize the spice level and toppings based on your preferences.

Lemon Garlic Shrimp with Quinoa

Ingredients:

For the Lemon Garlic Shrimp:

- 1 pound large shrimp, peeled and deveined
- 3 tablespoons olive oil
- 4 cloves garlic, minced
- Zest of 1 lemon
- Juice of 1 lemon
- 1 teaspoon dried oregano
- Salt and black pepper, to taste
- Crushed red pepper flakes, to taste (optional)
- Fresh parsley, chopped, for garnish

For the Quinoa:

- 1 cup quinoa, rinsed
- 2 cups water or vegetable broth
- Salt, to taste

Instructions:

Quinoa:

In a medium saucepan, combine quinoa and water or vegetable broth. Add salt to taste.
Bring to a boil, then reduce heat to low, cover, and simmer for 15-20 minutes or until the quinoa is cooked and the liquid is absorbed.
Fluff the quinoa with a fork and set aside.

Lemon Garlic Shrimp:

In a large skillet or pan, heat olive oil over medium heat.
Add minced garlic and sauté for 1-2 minutes until fragrant.
Add the shrimp to the skillet, spreading them out in an even layer.

Cook the shrimp for 2-3 minutes on one side until they start to turn pink.
Flip the shrimp and cook for an additional 2-3 minutes until they are opaque and cooked through.
Add lemon zest, lemon juice, dried oregano, salt, black pepper, and crushed red pepper flakes (if using) to the skillet. Toss the shrimp to coat them evenly in the lemon-garlic mixture.
Cook for an additional 1-2 minutes until the flavors meld and the shrimp are fully cooked.
Remove the skillet from the heat.

Assembly:

Serve the Lemon Garlic Shrimp over a bed of cooked quinoa.
Garnish with chopped fresh parsley.
Optionally, squeeze additional lemon juice over the dish before serving.
Enjoy the Lemon Garlic Shrimp with Quinoa hot.

This dish is a delightful combination of citrusy, garlicky shrimp and fluffy quinoa. It's a quick and easy meal that's perfect for a light lunch or dinner. Adjust the seasonings and spice level to suit your taste preferences.

Cabbage and Carrot Slaw with Grilled Chicken

Ingredients:

For the Grilled Chicken:

- 4 boneless, skinless chicken breasts
- 2 tablespoons olive oil
- 1 teaspoon smoked paprika
- 1 teaspoon garlic powder
- 1 teaspoon onion powder
- Salt and black pepper, to taste
- Lemon wedges, for serving (optional)

For the Cabbage and Carrot Slaw:

- 1/2 small green cabbage, thinly sliced
- 2 large carrots, grated
- 1/2 red onion, thinly sliced
- 1/4 cup fresh cilantro or parsley, chopped
- 1/4 cup mayonnaise
- 2 tablespoons Greek yogurt or sour cream
- 1 tablespoon Dijon mustard
- 1 tablespoon apple cider vinegar
- 1 tablespoon honey or maple syrup
- Salt and black pepper, to taste

Instructions:

Grilled Chicken:

Preheat the grill or grill pan over medium-high heat.
In a bowl, mix olive oil, smoked paprika, garlic powder, onion powder, salt, and black pepper to create a marinade.
Brush the chicken breasts with the marinade on both sides.
Grill the chicken for 6-8 minutes per side or until the internal temperature reaches 165°F (74°C) and the chicken is cooked through.

Remove the chicken from the grill and let it rest for a few minutes before slicing.

Cabbage and Carrot Slaw:

In a large bowl, combine sliced green cabbage, grated carrots, sliced red onion, and chopped cilantro or parsley.

In a separate small bowl, whisk together mayonnaise, Greek yogurt or sour cream, Dijon mustard, apple cider vinegar, honey or maple syrup, salt, and black pepper to create the dressing.

Pour the dressing over the cabbage mixture and toss until everything is well coated.

Assembly:

Serve the Grilled Chicken slices over a generous portion of Cabbage and Carrot Slaw.

Optionally, squeeze fresh lemon juice over the chicken before serving.

Enjoy the Cabbage and Carrot Slaw with Grilled Chicken as a refreshing and satisfying meal.

This Cabbage and Carrot Slaw with Grilled Chicken is a perfect combination of crunchy vegetables, tender grilled chicken, and a flavorful dressing. It's a light and wholesome dish that's great for lunch or dinner. Customize the slaw with your favorite herbs and adjust the dressing to suit your taste preferences.

Broccoli and Cheddar Stuffed Potatoes

Ingredients:

- 4 large baking potatoes
- 2 cups broccoli florets, steamed
- 1 cup shredded cheddar cheese
- 1/2 cup sour cream
- 2 tablespoons butter
- Salt and black pepper, to taste
- Chopped chives or green onions, for garnish (optional)

Instructions:

Preheat the oven to 400°F (200°C).

Wash and scrub the baking potatoes. Pierce each potato several times with a fork to allow steam to escape during baking.

Place the potatoes directly on the oven rack and bake for 45-60 minutes or until the potatoes are tender when pierced with a fork.

While the potatoes are baking, steam the broccoli florets until they are tender. You can steam them on the stovetop or in the microwave.

Once the potatoes are done, remove them from the oven and let them cool slightly.

Cut a lengthwise slit in the top of each potato, being careful not to cut all the way through.

Use a spoon to scoop out the flesh from each potato, leaving a thin layer attached to the skin to form a shell.

Place the scooped-out potato flesh in a bowl and mash it with a fork or potato masher.

Add steamed broccoli, shredded cheddar cheese, sour cream, butter, salt, and black pepper to the mashed potatoes. Mix until well combined.

Spoon the broccoli and cheddar filling back into the potato shells, dividing it evenly among them.

Place the stuffed potatoes back in the oven for 10-15 minutes or until the filling is heated through, and the cheese is melted and bubbly.

Remove from the oven and garnish with chopped chives or green onions if desired.

Serve the Broccoli and Cheddar Stuffed Potatoes hot as a delicious and satisfying side dish or main course.

These Broccoli and Cheddar Stuffed Potatoes make for a hearty and flavorful meal. Customize the filling with your favorite ingredients, such as bacon bits or additional herbs, to suit your taste preferences. Enjoy these stuffed potatoes for a comforting and wholesome dinner.

Turkey and Vegetable Skillet Lasagna

Ingredients:

- 1 pound ground turkey
- 1 onion, finely chopped
- 2 cloves garlic, minced
- 1 bell pepper, diced
- 1 zucchini, diced
- 1 carrot, grated
- 1 can (14 ounces) crushed tomatoes
- 1 can (14 ounces) diced tomatoes
- 2 tablespoons tomato paste
- 1 teaspoon dried oregano
- 1 teaspoon dried basil
- 1/2 teaspoon dried thyme
- Salt and black pepper, to taste
- 8 lasagna noodles, broken into smaller pieces
- 1 cup ricotta cheese
- 1 cup shredded mozzarella cheese
- Fresh basil or parsley, chopped, for garnish

Instructions:

In a large skillet or sauté pan, brown the ground turkey over medium heat, breaking it apart with a spoon as it cooks.
Add chopped onion and minced garlic to the skillet, sautéing until the onion is softened.
Stir in diced bell pepper, diced zucchini, and grated carrot. Cook for an additional 3-4 minutes until the vegetables start to soften.
Add crushed tomatoes, diced tomatoes, and tomato paste to the skillet. Mix well.
Season the mixture with dried oregano, dried basil, dried thyme, salt, and black pepper. Adjust the seasonings to taste.
Break the lasagna noodles into smaller pieces and stir them into the skillet, ensuring they are well coated in the sauce.
Cover the skillet and simmer for about 15-20 minutes or until the noodles are cooked al dente.

Dollop spoonfuls of ricotta cheese over the lasagna mixture. Sprinkle shredded mozzarella cheese on top.
Cover the skillet again and let it cook for an additional 5-7 minutes until the cheeses are melted and bubbly.
Garnish with chopped fresh basil or parsley.
Serve the Turkey and Vegetable Skillet Lasagna hot, directly from the skillet.

This Turkey and Vegetable Skillet Lasagna is a convenient and delicious way to enjoy the flavors of lasagna with minimal effort. The one-pan cooking method makes it a great option for a quick and satisfying weeknight dinner. Adjust the vegetable mix and cheese according to your preferences.

Baked Pesto Chicken

Ingredients:

- 4 boneless, skinless chicken breasts
- Salt and pepper to taste
- 1 cup pesto sauce (store-bought or homemade)
- 1 cup cherry tomatoes, halved
- 1 cup mozzarella cheese, shredded
- Fresh basil leaves for garnish (optional)

Instructions:

> Preheat your oven to 375°F (190°C).
> Season the chicken breasts with salt and pepper on both sides.
> Place the chicken breasts in a baking dish or on a lined baking sheet.
> Spread a generous layer of pesto sauce over each chicken breast.
> Scatter the halved cherry tomatoes around the chicken.
> Sprinkle the shredded mozzarella cheese evenly over the chicken and tomatoes.
> Bake in the preheated oven for about 25-30 minutes or until the chicken is cooked through and the cheese is melted and golden brown.
> If you prefer a more golden and bubbly cheese topping, you can broil the dish for an additional 2-3 minutes, but be sure to watch it closely to prevent burning.
> Once the chicken is done, remove it from the oven and let it rest for a few minutes.
> Garnish with fresh basil leaves, if desired.

Serve the baked pesto chicken with your favorite side dishes, such as rice, pasta, or a green salad. This dish is not only flavorful but also visually appealing, making it a great option for both casual family dinners and more special occasions.

Zucchini Noodles with Tomato Sauce and Turkey Meatballs

Ingredients:

For Turkey Meatballs:

- 1 pound ground turkey
- 1/2 cup breadcrumbs
- 1/4 cup grated Parmesan cheese
- 1/4 cup chopped fresh parsley
- 1 egg
- 2 cloves garlic, minced
- Salt and pepper to taste

For Zucchini Noodles:

- 4 medium-sized zucchini, spiralized into noodles
- 2 tablespoons olive oil
- Salt and pepper to taste

For Tomato Sauce:

- 1 can (28 ounces) crushed tomatoes
- 2 cloves garlic, minced
- 1 teaspoon dried oregano
- 1 teaspoon dried basil
- Salt and pepper to taste

Instructions:

1. Preheat the oven:

Preheat your oven to 400°F (200°C).

2. Make the Turkey Meatballs:

a. In a large bowl, combine ground turkey, breadcrumbs, Parmesan cheese, chopped parsley, egg, minced garlic, salt, and pepper.

b. Mix until well combined.

c. Shape the mixture into small meatballs and place them on a baking sheet lined with parchment paper.

d. Bake in the preheated oven for about 15-20 minutes or until the meatballs are cooked through and browned on the outside.

3. Prepare the Zucchini Noodles:

a. Spiralize the zucchini into noodles using a spiralizer.

b. Heat olive oil in a large skillet over medium heat.

c. Add the zucchini noodles to the skillet and sauté for 2-3 minutes until just tender.

d. Season with salt and pepper.

4. Make the Tomato Sauce:

a. In a saucepan, combine crushed tomatoes, minced garlic, dried oregano, dried basil, salt, and pepper.

b. Simmer the sauce over medium heat for about 10-15 minutes, stirring occasionally.

5. Assemble the Dish:

a. Toss the zucchini noodles with the tomato sauce until well coated.

b. Serve the zucchini noodles on plates, topped with the turkey meatballs.

c. Garnish with additional Parmesan cheese and fresh parsley if desired.

This zucchini noodle dish is not only delicious but also a nutritious and gluten-free option. It's a perfect meal for those looking to incorporate more vegetables and lean proteins into their diet.

Grilled Veggie Quesadillas

Ingredients:

- 2 large bell peppers (any color), sliced
- 1 large red onion, sliced
- 1 zucchini, sliced
- 1 yellow squash, sliced
- 1 cup cherry tomatoes, halved
- 2 tablespoons olive oil
- Salt and pepper to taste
- 4 large flour tortillas
- 2 cups shredded cheese (Mexican blend, cheddar, or your favorite melting cheese)
- 1/2 cup fresh cilantro, chopped (optional)
- Salsa, guacamole, or sour cream for serving (optional)

Instructions:

1. Preheat the Grill:

Preheat your grill to medium-high heat.

2. Prepare the Vegetables:

a. In a large bowl, toss the sliced bell peppers, red onion, zucchini, yellow squash, and cherry tomatoes with olive oil.

b. Season with salt and pepper to taste.

3. Grill the Vegetables:

a. Place the seasoned vegetables on the preheated grill grates.

b. Grill for 5-7 minutes, turning occasionally, until the vegetables are tender and slightly charred.

c. Remove the grilled vegetables from the grill and set aside.

4. Assemble the Quesadillas:

a. Lay out the flour tortillas on a clean surface.

b. Sprinkle a portion of shredded cheese evenly over one half of each tortilla.

c. Distribute the grilled vegetables over the cheese.

d. If desired, sprinkle chopped cilantro over the vegetables.

e. Fold the tortillas in half, pressing down gently.

5. Grill the Quesadillas:

a. Place the assembled quesadillas on the grill grates.

b. Grill for 2-3 minutes per side, or until the tortillas are golden brown and the cheese is melted.

6. Serve:

a. Remove the quesadillas from the grill and let them cool for a minute.

b. Slice each quesadilla into wedges and serve with salsa, guacamole, or sour cream on the side if desired.

Grilled Veggie Quesadillas make for a delicious and versatile meal. Feel free to customize them with your favorite vegetables, cheese, and toppings. They are perfect for a quick lunch, dinner, or even as a crowd-pleasing appetizer for gatherings.

Sweet and Spicy Glazed Salmon

Ingredients:

For the Glaze:

- 1/4 cup soy sauce
- 2 tablespoons honey
- 1 tablespoon Dijon mustard
- 1 tablespoon Sriracha sauce (adjust to taste for desired spice level)
- 2 cloves garlic, minced
- 1 teaspoon grated ginger
- 1 tablespoon olive oil

For the Salmon:

- 4 salmon fillets (about 6 ounces each), skin-on or skinless
- Salt and pepper to taste
- 1 tablespoon olive oil
- Sesame seeds and chopped green onions for garnish (optional)

Instructions:

1. Preheat the Oven:

Preheat your oven to 400°F (200°C).

2. Make the Glaze:

a. In a small saucepan, combine soy sauce, honey, Dijon mustard, Sriracha sauce, minced garlic, grated ginger, and olive oil.

b. Heat the mixture over medium heat, stirring continuously until it comes to a simmer.

c. Reduce the heat to low and let it simmer for 2-3 minutes until the glaze thickens slightly. Remove from heat.

3. Prepare the Salmon:

a. Pat the salmon fillets dry with paper towels.

b. Season both sides of the salmon fillets with salt and pepper.

4. Sear the Salmon:

a. Heat olive oil in an oven-safe skillet over medium-high heat.

b. Place the salmon fillets in the skillet, skin side down if skin-on.

c. Sear for 2-3 minutes until the salmon gets a golden crust.

5. Glaze the Salmon:

a. Brush the glaze over the salmon fillets, coating them evenly.

b. If using an oven-safe skillet, transfer the skillet to the preheated oven. Otherwise, transfer the salmon to a baking dish.

6. Bake the Salmon:

a. Bake in the preheated oven for 8-10 minutes, or until the salmon is cooked through and flakes easily with a fork.

7. Garnish and Serve:

a. Remove the salmon from the oven.

b. Garnish with sesame seeds and chopped green onions, if desired.

c. Serve the sweet and spicy glazed salmon over rice or with your favorite side dishes.

This Sweet and Spicy Glazed Salmon is perfect for a quick and flavorful dinner. The glaze adds a nice balance of sweetness and heat to the rich salmon flavor.

Mediterranean Quinoa Bowl

Ingredients:

For the Quinoa Bowl:

- 1 cup quinoa, rinsed
- 2 cups water or vegetable broth
- 1 cup cherry tomatoes, halved
- 1 cucumber, diced
- 1 bell pepper (red, yellow, or orange), diced
- 1/2 red onion, finely chopped
- 1/2 cup Kalamata olives, pitted and sliced
- 1/2 cup crumbled feta cheese
- 1/4 cup fresh parsley, chopped
- Salt and pepper to taste

For the Dressing:

- 1/4 cup extra-virgin olive oil
- 2 tablespoons red wine vinegar
- 1 teaspoon Dijon mustard
- 1 clove garlic, minced
- 1 teaspoon dried oregano
- Salt and pepper to taste

Instructions:

1. Cook the Quinoa:

a. In a medium saucepan, combine the quinoa and water or vegetable broth.

b. Bring to a boil, then reduce the heat to low, cover, and simmer for 15-20 minutes, or until the quinoa is cooked and the liquid is absorbed.

c. Fluff the quinoa with a fork and let it cool to room temperature.

2. Prepare the Vegetables:

a. In a large mixing bowl, combine the cooked quinoa, cherry tomatoes, cucumber, bell pepper, red onion, Kalamata olives, feta cheese, and fresh parsley.

b. Toss the ingredients together until well combined.

c. Season with salt and pepper to taste.

3. Make the Dressing:

a. In a small bowl, whisk together the olive oil, red wine vinegar, Dijon mustard, minced garlic, dried oregano, salt, and pepper.

4. Assemble the Mediterranean Quinoa Bowl:

a. Pour the dressing over the quinoa and vegetable mixture.

b. Toss everything together until the ingredients are evenly coated with the dressing.

5. Serve:

a. Divide the Mediterranean quinoa mixture into bowls.

b. Garnish with additional feta cheese and parsley if desired.

c. Serve immediately and enjoy your healthy and delicious Mediterranean Quinoa Bowl.

Feel free to customize this recipe by adding grilled chicken, chickpeas, or other Mediterranean-inspired ingredients to suit your taste. It's a versatile and satisfying dish that works well for lunch or dinner.

Chicken and Vegetable Curry

Ingredients:

- 1.5 lbs (700g) boneless, skinless chicken thighs, cut into bite-sized pieces
- 2 tablespoons vegetable oil
- 1 large onion, finely chopped
- 3 cloves garlic, minced
- 1 tablespoon ginger, grated
- 1-2 tablespoons curry powder (adjust to taste)
- 1 teaspoon ground cumin
- 1 teaspoon ground coriander
- 1 teaspoon turmeric
- 1/2 teaspoon chili powder (adjust to taste)
- 1 can (14 oz/400g) diced tomatoes
- 1 can (14 oz/400ml) coconut milk
- 2 large carrots, peeled and sliced
- 1 large bell pepper, chopped
- 1 cup (150g) green beans, trimmed and cut into bite-sized pieces
- Salt and pepper to taste
- Fresh cilantro, chopped, for garnish
- Cooked rice or naan bread for serving

Instructions:

Prepare the Chicken:
- Season the chicken pieces with salt and pepper.
- In a large skillet or Dutch oven, heat the vegetable oil over medium-high heat.

Brown the Chicken:
- Add the chicken pieces to the skillet and brown them on all sides. Once browned, remove them from the skillet and set aside.

Sauté the Aromatics:
- In the same skillet, add a bit more oil if needed. Add the chopped onion and sauté until softened.
- Add minced garlic and grated ginger, sauté for another 1-2 minutes until fragrant.

Add the Spices:

- Stir in the curry powder, ground cumin, ground coriander, turmeric, and chili powder. Cook for 1-2 minutes to toast the spices.

Combine Tomatoes and Coconut Milk:
- Pour in the diced tomatoes with their juice and coconut milk. Stir well to combine.

Simmer the Curry:
- Add the browned chicken back to the skillet. Bring the mixture to a simmer, then reduce the heat to low, cover, and let it simmer for about 15-20 minutes or until the chicken is cooked through.

Add Vegetables:
- Add the sliced carrots, chopped bell pepper, and green beans. Simmer for an additional 10-15 minutes or until the vegetables are tender.

Adjust Seasoning:
- Taste the curry and adjust the seasoning with salt and pepper as needed.

Serve:
- Serve the chicken and vegetable curry over cooked rice or with naan bread.
- Garnish with fresh chopped cilantro.

Enjoy your homemade chicken and vegetable curry! Feel free to adjust the spice levels and vegetable selection based on your preferences.

Cauliflower and Chickpea Tacos

Ingredients:

For the Cauliflower and Chickpea Filling:

- 1 small head cauliflower, cut into small florets
- 1 can (15 oz) chickpeas, drained and rinsed
- 2 tablespoons olive oil
- 1 teaspoon ground cumin
- 1 teaspoon smoked paprika
- 1/2 teaspoon chili powder
- 1/2 teaspoon garlic powder
- Salt and pepper to taste

For the Cilantro Lime Crema:

- 1/2 cup Greek yogurt or sour cream
- 2 tablespoons fresh cilantro, chopped
- 1 tablespoon lime juice
- Salt to taste

For Assembling Tacos:

- Small tortillas (corn or flour)
- Shredded lettuce
- Diced tomatoes
- Sliced red onion
- Avocado slices
- Crumbled feta or cotija cheese (optional)
- Lime wedges for serving

Instructions:

1. Preheat the Oven:

    - Preheat your oven to 400°F (200°C).

2. Roast the Cauliflower and Chickpeas:

a. In a large bowl, toss the cauliflower florets and chickpeas with olive oil, ground cumin, smoked paprika, chili powder, garlic powder, salt, and pepper until well coated.

b. Spread the mixture on a baking sheet lined with parchment paper.

c. Roast in the preheated oven for about 20-25 minutes or until the cauliflower is tender and golden brown, stirring halfway through.

3. Prepare the Cilantro Lime Crema:

- In a small bowl, mix together Greek yogurt or sour cream, chopped cilantro, lime juice, and salt. Adjust the seasoning to taste.

4. Assemble the Tacos:

a. Warm the tortillas according to package instructions.

b. Spread a spoonful of the cilantro lime crema on each tortilla.

c. Add a generous portion of the roasted cauliflower and chickpea mixture.

d. Top with shredded lettuce, diced tomatoes, sliced red onion, avocado slices, and crumbled feta or cotija cheese if using.

5. Serve:

- Serve the cauliflower and chickpea tacos with lime wedges on the side.
- Enjoy your delicious and flavorful vegetarian tacos!

Feel free to customize your tacos with additional toppings like salsa, hot sauce, or your favorite fresh herbs. These tacos are a great way to enjoy a meatless meal that is both tasty and satisfying.

Turkey and Sweet Potato Hash

Ingredients:

- 1 pound ground turkey
- 2 large sweet potatoes, peeled and diced into small cubes
- 1 onion, finely chopped
- 2 cloves garlic, minced
- 1 bell pepper, diced (any color)
- 2 tablespoons olive oil
- 1 teaspoon ground cumin
- 1 teaspoon paprika
- 1/2 teaspoon chili powder (optional, for added heat)
- Salt and pepper to taste
- Fresh parsley or green onions for garnish (optional)
- Fried or poached eggs for serving (optional)

Instructions:

1. Cook the Sweet Potatoes:

- In a large skillet, heat the olive oil over medium heat.
- Add the diced sweet potatoes to the skillet and cook until they are tender, stirring occasionally. This will take about 10-15 minutes.

2. Brown the Turkey:

- Push the sweet potatoes to the side of the skillet and add ground turkey to the empty space.
- Break up the turkey with a spatula and cook until browned.

3. Saute Vegetables:

- Add chopped onions, minced garlic, and diced bell pepper to the skillet. Cook until the vegetables are softened.

4. Season the Hash:

- Sprinkle ground cumin, paprika, chili powder (if using), salt, and pepper over the mixture. Stir well to combine, ensuring that the spices are evenly distributed.

5. Finish Cooking:

- Continue cooking the hash for an additional 5-7 minutes, stirring occasionally, until the sweet potatoes are fully cooked, and the flavors meld together.

6. Garnish and Serve:

- Garnish the turkey and sweet potato hash with fresh parsley or green onions if desired.
- Optionally, serve the hash with fried or poached eggs on top.

7. Serve Warm:

- Serve the turkey and sweet potato hash warm, either on its own or with your favorite hot sauce.

This dish is not only delicious but also a great way to enjoy a balanced and nutritious meal. The sweet potatoes add a natural sweetness, while the ground turkey provides lean protein. Customize the spices and toppings based on your preferences, and enjoy a satisfying meal for breakfast, brunch, or any time of the day!

Caprese Quinoa Salad

Ingredients:

For the Salad:

- 1 cup quinoa, rinsed
- 2 cups cherry tomatoes, halved
- 1 cup fresh mozzarella balls (bocconcini), halved
- 1/2 cup fresh basil leaves, torn
- Salt and pepper to taste

For the Dressing:

- 1/4 cup extra-virgin olive oil
- 2 tablespoons balsamic vinegar
- 1 teaspoon Dijon mustard
- 1 clove garlic, minced
- Salt and pepper to taste

Instructions:

1. Cook the Quinoa:

- In a medium saucepan, combine the quinoa with 2 cups of water. Bring to a boil, then reduce the heat to low, cover, and simmer for 15-20 minutes or until the quinoa is cooked and the water is absorbed. Fluff the quinoa with a fork and let it cool to room temperature.

2. Prepare the Dressing:

- In a small bowl, whisk together the olive oil, balsamic vinegar, Dijon mustard, minced garlic, salt, and pepper. Set aside.

3. Assemble the Salad:

- In a large mixing bowl, combine the cooked and cooled quinoa, cherry tomatoes, fresh mozzarella balls, and torn basil leaves.
- Season with salt and pepper to taste.

4. Add the Dressing:

- Pour the dressing over the salad ingredients.

5. Toss Gently:

- Gently toss the salad until all the ingredients are well coated with the dressing.

6. Chill (Optional):

- You can refrigerate the salad for about 30 minutes to allow the flavors to meld, or you can serve it immediately.

7. Serve:

- Serve the Caprese Quinoa Salad in a large bowl or individual plates.

This Caprese Quinoa Salad is perfect for a light and refreshing meal, whether as a side dish or a main course. It's a great option for picnics, potlucks, or a quick and healthy lunch. Adjust the quantities and ingredients to suit your preferences, and enjoy the delightful combination of flavors.

Lemon Garlic Roasted Chicken Thighs

Ingredients:

- 4-6 bone-in, skin-on chicken thighs
- Salt and black pepper to taste
- 2 tablespoons olive oil
- 4 cloves garlic, minced
- Zest of 1 lemon
- Juice of 1 lemon
- 1 teaspoon dried thyme (or 1 tablespoon fresh thyme leaves)
- 1 teaspoon dried rosemary
- 1 teaspoon paprika
- Fresh parsley for garnish (optional)
- Lemon wedges for serving

Instructions:

1. Preheat the Oven:

- Preheat your oven to 400°F (200°C).

2. Season the Chicken:

- Pat the chicken thighs dry with paper towels.
- Season both sides of the chicken thighs with salt and black pepper.

3. Make the Lemon Garlic Mixture:

- In a small bowl, combine olive oil, minced garlic, lemon zest, lemon juice, dried thyme, dried rosemary, and paprika. Mix well.

4. Coat the Chicken:

- Place the chicken thighs in a large bowl or a Ziploc bag.

- Pour the lemon garlic mixture over the chicken thighs, making sure each piece is well coated. You can use your hands to massage the mixture into the chicken for even coverage.

5. Arrange in a Baking Dish:

- Place the chicken thighs in a baking dish, skin side up.

6. Roast in the Oven:

- Roast the chicken in the preheated oven for approximately 35-40 minutes or until the internal temperature reaches 165°F (74°C) and the skin is golden and crispy.

7. Baste the Chicken:

- If desired, baste the chicken with the pan juices halfway through the cooking time to keep it moist.

8. Garnish and Serve:

- Once the chicken is cooked, remove it from the oven.
- Garnish with fresh parsley (if using) and serve the Lemon Garlic Roasted Chicken Thighs with lemon wedges on the side.

This dish pairs well with a variety of side dishes such as roasted vegetables, mashed potatoes, or a simple green salad. The lemon and garlic infuse the chicken with a bright and savory flavor, making it a delightful and easy-to-make meal.

Ratatouille

Ingredients:

- 1 large eggplant, sliced into rounds
- 2 medium zucchini, sliced into rounds
- 1 large bell pepper (red or yellow), sliced
- 4 medium tomatoes, sliced
- 1 onion, thinly sliced
- 3 cloves garlic, minced
- 2 tablespoons tomato paste
- 2 tablespoons olive oil
- 1 teaspoon dried thyme
- 1 teaspoon dried oregano
- Salt and black pepper to taste
- Fresh basil or parsley for garnish (optional)

Instructions:

1. Prepare the Vegetables:

- Preheat the oven to 375°F (190°C).
- Arrange the sliced eggplant, zucchini, bell pepper, and tomatoes in overlapping rows, either in a circular pattern or in a straight line, in a large baking dish.

2. Make the Tomato Sauce:

- In a small bowl, mix together the minced garlic, tomato paste, olive oil, dried thyme, dried oregano, salt, and black pepper.

3. Assemble and Bake:

- Drizzle the tomato sauce over the arranged vegetables in the baking dish, ensuring that each slice is coated.
- Cover the baking dish with aluminum foil and bake in the preheated oven for 40-45 minutes.

4. Uncover and Finish Baking:

- Remove the foil and bake for an additional 15-20 minutes, or until the vegetables are tender and slightly caramelized on the edges.

5. Garnish and Serve:

- Remove from the oven and let it cool slightly.
- Garnish with fresh basil or parsley if desired.
- Serve the Ratatouille warm as a side dish, over rice, pasta, or with a crusty baguette.

Ratatouille is not only a tasty and vibrant dish but also a great way to enjoy the flavors of fresh, seasonal vegetables. This recipe allows you to savor the rich and aromatic essence of the Mediterranean cuisine.

Sesame Ginger Tofu Stir-Fry

Ingredients:

For the Tofu:

- 14 oz (400g) extra-firm tofu, pressed and cubed
- 2 tablespoons soy sauce
- 1 tablespoon sesame oil
- 1 tablespoon cornstarch
- 1 tablespoon vegetable oil (for cooking)

For the Stir-Fry:

- 1 tablespoon vegetable oil
- 1 bell pepper, thinly sliced
- 1 carrot, julienned or thinly sliced
- 1 cup broccoli florets
- 2 cloves garlic, minced
- 1 tablespoon fresh ginger, grated
- 3 tablespoons soy sauce
- 1 tablespoon hoisin sauce
- 1 tablespoon rice vinegar
- 1 tablespoon sesame oil
- 1 tablespoon honey or maple syrup
- 1 tablespoon sesame seeds (for garnish)
- Green onions, chopped (for garnish)
- Cooked rice or noodles (for serving)

Instructions:

1. Prepare the Tofu:

- Press the tofu to remove excess water by wrapping it in a clean kitchen towel and placing a heavy object (like a book or skillet) on top. Leave it for 15-20 minutes.
- Cut the pressed tofu into cubes.
- In a bowl, mix soy sauce, sesame oil, and cornstarch. Add the tofu cubes to the mixture and toss until coated.

2. Cook the Tofu:

- Heat 1 tablespoon of vegetable oil in a large skillet or wok over medium-high heat.
- Add the tofu cubes and cook until they are golden brown on all sides. Remove from the pan and set aside.

3. Prepare the Stir-Fry:

- In the same skillet, add another tablespoon of vegetable oil.
- Add sliced bell pepper, julienned carrot, and broccoli florets. Stir-fry for 3-4 minutes or until the vegetables are tender-crisp.

4. Add Aromatics:

- Add minced garlic and grated ginger to the vegetables. Stir for about 1 minute until fragrant.

5. Make the Sauce:

- In a small bowl, whisk together soy sauce, hoisin sauce, rice vinegar, sesame oil, and honey or maple syrup.

6. Combine and Finish:

- Add the cooked tofu back to the skillet along with the prepared sauce.
- Toss everything together until well coated and heated through.

7. Serve:

- Serve the Sesame Ginger Tofu Stir-Fry over cooked rice or noodles.
- Garnish with sesame seeds and chopped green onions.

Enjoy this flavorful and nutritious tofu stir-fry as a satisfying and wholesome meal. Feel free to customize the vegetables and adjust the sauce according to your taste preferences.

Baked Eggplant Lasagna

Ingredients:

For the Eggplant Layers:

- 2 large eggplants, thinly sliced lengthwise
- Salt
- Olive oil for brushing

For the Meat Sauce:

- 1 lb (450g) ground beef or Italian sausage
- 1 onion, finely chopped
- 3 cloves garlic, minced
- 1 can (14 oz/400g) crushed tomatoes
- 1 can (14 oz/400g) tomato sauce
- 2 tablespoons tomato paste
- 1 teaspoon dried oregano
- 1 teaspoon dried basil
- Salt and pepper to taste

For the Cheese Filling:

- 2 cups ricotta cheese
- 1 cup mozzarella cheese, shredded
- 1/2 cup Parmesan cheese, grated
- 1 egg
- 2 tablespoons fresh basil, chopped
- Salt and pepper to taste

Instructions:

1. Preheat the Oven:

- Preheat your oven to 375°F (190°C).

2. Prepare the Eggplant:

- Sprinkle the eggplant slices with salt and let them sit for about 15-20 minutes. This helps draw out excess moisture.
- Rinse the eggplant slices and pat them dry with paper towels.
- Brush both sides of each eggplant slice with olive oil and place them on a baking sheet.
- Bake in the preheated oven for 15-20 minutes or until the eggplant slices are tender.

3. Make the Meat Sauce:

- In a large skillet, brown the ground beef or sausage over medium heat.
- Add chopped onion and minced garlic. Cook until the onion is softened.
- Stir in crushed tomatoes, tomato sauce, tomato paste, dried oregano, dried basil, salt, and pepper.
- Simmer the sauce for about 15-20 minutes to allow the flavors to meld.

4. Prepare the Cheese Filling:

- In a bowl, combine ricotta cheese, mozzarella cheese, Parmesan cheese, egg, chopped basil, salt, and pepper. Mix well.

5. Assemble the Lasagna:

- In a baking dish, start layering the ingredients: a thin layer of meat sauce, a layer of eggplant slices, and a layer of cheese filling.
- Repeat the layers until all ingredients are used, finishing with a layer of cheese on top.

6. Bake:

- Cover the baking dish with foil and bake in the preheated oven for 30 minutes.
- Remove the foil and bake for an additional 15-20 minutes or until the top is golden and bubbly.

7. Rest and Serve:

- Let the baked eggplant lasagna rest for 10-15 minutes before slicing.
- Serve and enjoy!

This Baked Eggplant Lasagna is a flavorful and satisfying dish that's sure to please both eggplant and lasagna enthusiasts. Adjust the seasoning and cheese quantities to suit your taste preferences.

Greek Yogurt Chicken Salad Wraps

Ingredients:

For the Chicken Salad:

- 2 cups cooked chicken breast, shredded or diced
- 1/2 cup Greek yogurt (plain, non-fat)
- 1/4 cup red onion, finely chopped
- 1/4 cup celery, finely chopped
- 1/4 cup cucumber, finely chopped
- 1/4 cup red bell pepper, finely chopped
- 1/4 cup kalamata olives, pitted and chopped
- 2 tablespoons fresh parsley, chopped
- 1 tablespoon lemon juice
- Salt and pepper to taste

For the Wraps:

- Whole-grain or spinach tortillas
- Fresh spinach leaves
- Tomato slices
- Feta cheese, crumbled (optional)

Instructions:

1. Make the Chicken Salad:

- In a large bowl, combine the cooked chicken, Greek yogurt, red onion, celery, cucumber, red bell pepper, kalamata olives, parsley, lemon juice, salt, and pepper.
- Mix well until all ingredients are evenly coated.

2. Assemble the Wraps:

- Lay out the tortillas on a clean surface.
- Place a few fresh spinach leaves in the center of each tortilla.
- Spoon the Greek yogurt chicken salad over the spinach.

- Add tomato slices and crumbled feta cheese if desired.

3. Wrap it Up:

- Fold in the sides of the tortilla and then roll it up tightly from the bottom, creating a wrap.

4. Serve:

- Slice the wraps in half diagonally if desired.
- Serve immediately and enjoy!

These Greek Yogurt Chicken Salad Wraps are perfect for a quick and healthy lunch or a light dinner. The Greek yogurt adds a creamy texture, while the combination of vegetables and olives provides a burst of freshness. Feel free to customize the recipe by adding other favorite ingredients such as avocado, sun-dried tomatoes, or different herbs.

Black Bean and Sweet Potato Enchiladas

Ingredients:

For the Filling:

- 2 medium sweet potatoes, peeled and diced
- 1 can (15 oz) black beans, drained and rinsed
- 1 cup corn kernels (fresh or frozen)
- 1 red bell pepper, diced
- 1 small red onion, finely chopped
- 2 cloves garlic, minced
- 1 teaspoon ground cumin
- 1 teaspoon chili powder
- Salt and pepper to taste
- 1 tablespoon olive oil

For the Enchilada Sauce:

- 2 cups tomato sauce
- 1 cup vegetable broth
- 2 teaspoons ground cumin
- 2 teaspoons chili powder
- 1 teaspoon garlic powder
- 1 teaspoon onion powder
- Salt and pepper to taste

For Assembly:

- 8 large whole-grain or corn tortillas
- 2 cups shredded Mexican blend cheese
- Fresh cilantro, chopped, for garnish
- Avocado slices, for serving (optional)
- Sour cream or Greek yogurt, for serving (optional)

Instructions:

1. Roast the Sweet Potatoes:

   - Preheat the oven to 400°F (200°C).
   - Toss the diced sweet potatoes with olive oil, ground cumin, chili powder, salt, and pepper.
   - Spread the sweet potatoes on a baking sheet and roast for about 20-25 minutes or until tender.

2. Make the Filling:

   - In a large bowl, combine the roasted sweet potatoes, black beans, corn, red bell pepper, red onion, garlic, cumin, chili powder, salt, and pepper. Mix well.

3. Prepare the Enchilada Sauce:

   - In a saucepan, combine tomato sauce, vegetable broth, ground cumin, chili powder, garlic powder, onion powder, salt, and pepper. Bring to a simmer and cook for 5-7 minutes.

4. Assemble the Enchiladas:

   - Spread a small amount of enchilada sauce on the bottom of a baking dish.
   - Warm the tortillas briefly in the microwave to make them pliable.
   - Spoon the filling mixture onto each tortilla, roll them up, and place them seam side down in the baking dish.

5. Pour the Sauce:

   - Pour the remaining enchilada sauce over the rolled tortillas.

6. Add Cheese and Bake:

   - Sprinkle shredded cheese over the top of the enchiladas.
   - Bake in the preheated oven for 20-25 minutes or until the cheese is melted and bubbly.

7. Serve:

- Garnish the enchiladas with chopped cilantro.
- Serve with avocado slices and a dollop of sour cream or Greek yogurt if desired.

These Black Bean and Sweet Potato Enchiladas are a flavorful and nutritious option for a meatless meal. Feel free to customize the recipe with additional toppings such as salsa, guacamole, or lime wedges.

Pesto and Vegetable Pizza with Whole Wheat Crust

Ingredients:

For the Whole Wheat Pizza Dough:

- 2 1/4 teaspoons (1 packet) active dry yeast
- 1 cup warm water (110°F/43°C)
- 1 tablespoon honey or maple syrup
- 2 1/2 cups whole wheat flour
- 1 tablespoon olive oil
- 1/2 teaspoon salt

For the Pesto Sauce:

- 2 cups fresh basil leaves, packed
- 1/2 cup grated Parmesan cheese
- 1/2 cup pine nuts or walnuts
- 2 cloves garlic, minced
- 1/2 cup extra-virgin olive oil
- Salt and pepper to taste

For the Pizza Toppings:

- 1 cup cherry tomatoes, halved
- 1 bell pepper, thinly sliced
- 1 zucchini, thinly sliced
- 1/2 red onion, thinly sliced
- 1 cup shredded mozzarella cheese
- 1/4 cup grated Parmesan cheese
- Red pepper flakes (optional)
- Fresh basil leaves for garnish

Instructions:

1. Prepare the Whole Wheat Pizza Dough:

- In a small bowl, combine warm water, honey (or maple syrup), and yeast. Let it sit for about 5 minutes until the mixture becomes frothy.
- In a large mixing bowl, combine whole wheat flour, olive oil, and salt.

- Add the yeast mixture to the flour mixture and knead until a dough forms.
- Place the dough in a lightly oiled bowl, cover with a damp cloth, and let it rise in a warm place for about 1 hour or until it doubles in size.

2. Make the Pesto Sauce:

- In a food processor, combine fresh basil, grated Parmesan cheese, pine nuts (or walnuts), minced garlic, olive oil, salt, and pepper.
- Process until the mixture reaches a smooth consistency.

3. Preheat the Oven:

- Preheat your oven to 450°F (230°C).

4. Roll Out the Dough:

- On a floured surface, roll out the whole wheat pizza dough to your desired thickness.

5. Assemble the Pizza:

- Transfer the rolled-out dough to a pizza stone or baking sheet.
- Spread the pesto sauce evenly over the dough.
- Sprinkle with shredded mozzarella cheese, followed by cherry tomatoes, bell pepper, zucchini, and red onion.
- Finish with a sprinkle of grated Parmesan cheese.

6. Bake:

- Bake in the preheated oven for 15-20 minutes or until the crust is golden and the cheese is bubbly and slightly browned.

7. Garnish and Serve:

- Remove the pizza from the oven and let it cool for a few minutes.
- Garnish with red pepper flakes (if desired) and fresh basil leaves.
- Slice and serve your Pesto and Vegetable Pizza with Whole Wheat Crust.

Enjoy a tasty and nutritious pizza with the goodness of whole wheat crust and a flavorful pesto sauce loaded with fresh vegetables. Feel free to customize the toppings based on your preferences!

Roasted Red Pepper and Lentil Soup

Ingredients:

- 2 large red bell peppers, halved and seeds removed
- 1 cup dried red lentils, rinsed and drained
- 1 onion, chopped
- 2 carrots, peeled and chopped
- 2 celery stalks, chopped
- 3 cloves garlic, minced
- 1 can (14 oz) crushed tomatoes
- 4 cups vegetable broth
- 1 teaspoon ground cumin
- 1 teaspoon smoked paprika
- 1/2 teaspoon ground coriander
- 1/4 teaspoon cayenne pepper (optional, for heat)
- Salt and black pepper to taste
- 2 tablespoons olive oil
- Fresh cilantro or parsley for garnish
- Lemon wedges for serving

Instructions:

1. Roast the Red Peppers:

- Preheat your oven's broiler.
- Place the red pepper halves, skin side up, on a baking sheet.
- Broil the peppers until the skins are charred and blistered, about 8-10 minutes.
- Remove from the oven, place the peppers in a bowl, cover with plastic wrap, and let them steam for about 10 minutes.
- Peel off the charred skins and chop the roasted peppers.

2. Cook the Lentils:

- In a large pot, heat olive oil over medium heat.
- Add onions, carrots, celery, and garlic. Sauté until the vegetables are softened, about 5 minutes.

- Stir in cumin, smoked paprika, ground coriander, and cayenne pepper (if using).
- Add crushed tomatoes, roasted red peppers, red lentils, and vegetable broth. Season with salt and black pepper.

3. Simmer the Soup:

- Bring the soup to a boil, then reduce the heat to low, cover, and simmer for about 20-25 minutes or until the lentils are tender.

4. Blend the Soup:

- Use an immersion blender to blend the soup until smooth. Alternatively, transfer the soup in batches to a blender, blend until smooth, and return to the pot.

5. Adjust Seasoning:

- Taste and adjust the seasoning if necessary. Add more salt, pepper, or spices to suit your preferences.

6. Serve:

- Ladle the soup into bowls.
- Garnish with fresh cilantro or parsley.
- Serve with lemon wedges on the side.

Enjoy your Roasted Red Pepper and Lentil Soup with a slice of crusty bread for a wholesome and satisfying meal. The roasted red peppers add depth to the flavor, while the lentils provide a hearty and nutritious base.

www.ingramcontent.com/pod-product-compliance
Lightning Source LLC
LaVergne TN
LVHW081600060526
838201LV00054B/1991